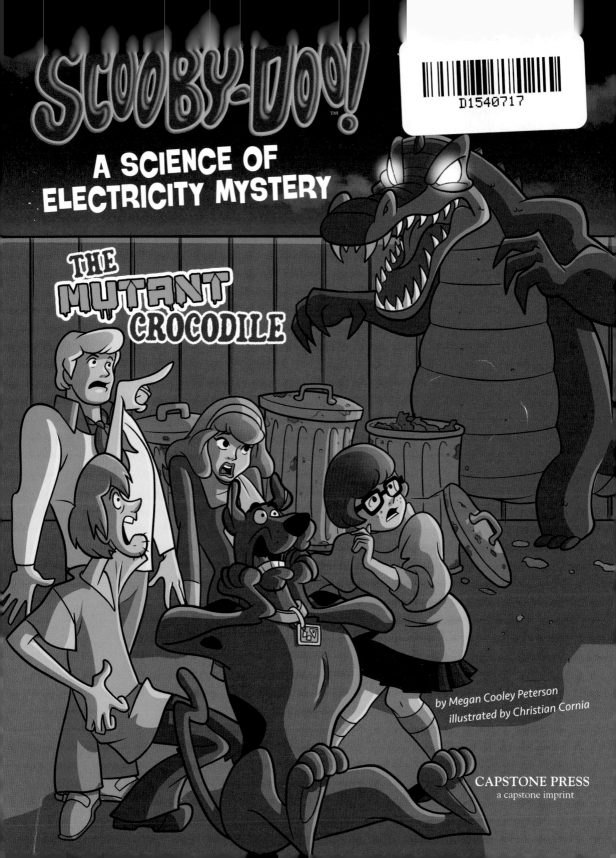

SCOOBY-DOO!

A SCIENCE OF ELECTRICITY MYSTERY

THE MUTANT CROCODILE

by Megan Cooley Peterson

illustrated by Christian Cornia

CAPSTONE PRESS
a capstone imprint

"Jinkies!" said Velma. "That is one spooky monster!"

"Rouch!" said Scooby, jumping off the rug.

"I, like, totally shocked Scoob!" exclaimed Shaggy. "The monster movie gave me monster powers!"

"It's static electricity," Daphne explained. "Not monster powers."

"Daphne's right," said Fred. "Static electricity is electricity that collects on an object's surface."

"Electrical energy starts with an atom," continued Velma. "Inside the atom's nucleus are protons and neutrons. Protons have a positive electrical charge. Neutrons have no electrical charge."

"Electrons spin around the atom's nucleus," added Daphne. "They have a negative electrical charge. Charges that are the same, such as two positives, repel each other. Opposite charges, like a positive and negative charge, attract."

"When you dragged your socks across the rug, electrons from the rug's atoms jumped into your socks' atoms," Fred said. "Those extra electrons gave you a negative charge."

"And then you touched Scooby," said Velma. "A bunch of your extra electrons jumped over to him and created a spark."

"So, like, is static electricity the same kind of electricity that powers the TV?" Shaggy asked.

"Not exactly," said Fred. "Static electricity builds up in one place. Dynamic electricity, like in a television, is the steady flow of electrons. That flow of electrons is called an electrical current."

"Electrons need something to flow through, called a conductor," Daphne said.

"A conductor?" asked Shaggy. "I thought conductors told the orchestra how to play music."

"Rusic!" agreed Scooby.

"We're talking about conductors that help electrons flow. Metals are good conductors," Velma said.

Scooby unplugged the lamp, looking for electricity.

"You can't see the electricty, Scooby," said Velma. "But that electrical cord is part of a circuit. When you turn on a device, electricity flows through the device, completing the circuit."

"A circuit is a loop of wires," Fred added. "Electricity flows through the circuit and back out again. All parts of the circuit must be connected. If the circuit is broken, the flow of electricity stops. The device turns off."

"Thanks for the science lesson, Scooby-Doo!" exclaimed Shaggy.

"Rou're relcome!" said Scooby.

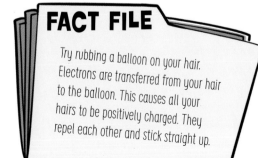

FACT FILE

Try rubbing a balloon on your hair. Electrons are transferred from your hair to the balloon. This causes all your hairs to be positively charged. They repel each other and stick straight up.

"Now the TV's off too. Did you unplug everything, Scoob?" Shaggy asked. "Scooby-Doo, where are you?"

"Right rere!" Scooby said.

"The power must be out," said Velma. "Electricity travels from the power plant through power lines. Maybe one of the lines is down?"

"You might be right," Daphne said. "Power lines are large-scale conductors. A damaged line cuts off the electrical current."

"Did you hear that?" Fred asked.

"Something, or someone, is rooting around in those garbage cans," Velma said. "Let's check it out."

"Here we go again," groaned Shaggy.

FACT FILE

Power grids move electricity from power plants to homes and businesses through power lines and facilities called substations. Substations increase the voltage to be able to travel long distances throughout the grid and then decrease the voltage for use in our homes.

"Zoinks!" exclaimed Shaggy. **"It's a monster crocodile!"**

"Rocodile!" shouted Scooby.

"That's one creepy reptile," said Daphne.

"I bet it's more scared of us that we are of it," Velma added. "It was sure in a hurry to get away."

Fred picked up a potato. "Look at this pile of potatoes, gang," he said.

"French fries are made from potatoes," Shaggy noted. "That crocodile has excellent taste in snack foods."

"That's our compost barrel," Velma said. "We throw old vegetables in it. Maybe the crocodile was looking for scraps to eat."

"There's a document near the potatoes," noticed Daphne. "It's got the power plant's logo on it. I wonder how it got here?"

"Are you thinking what I'm thinking?" Velma asked.

"I sure am. Tomorrow we're going to the power plant!" said Fred.

"Look!" cried Shaggy. "The power plant is, like, totally on fire!"

"This power plant burns coal," Fred said. "That smoke you see is from the burning coal."

"So, like, how does burning coal make electricity?" Shaggy asked.

"The heat from the burning coal boils water," Daphne explained. "The boiling water creates strong bursts of steam. The steam turns the blades of a turbine."

"When the turbine moves, it turns a generator," Velma continued. "Inside the generator, magnets spin inside wire coils. This causes an electric current to appear in the coils. The current then flows into a conducting wire. That's how electricity is created."

"Velma's right," said Fred. "The motion of the spinning magnets produces energy in the form of an electrical current inside the wire. Generators convert the mechanical energy of the turbine and the spinning magnets into electrical energy."

"Motors work the opposite way," Velma added. "Motors take electrical or chemical energy and change it into mechanical energy to make things move."

"Do all power plants burn coal?" Shaggy asked.

"Coal is a fossil fuel," Daphne said. "Some plants burn other kinds of fossil fuels, like oil or natural gas."

"Fossils fuels can't be renewed," Fred said. "Once they're gone, they're gone. And burning them causes pollution."

"Let's go talk to that group of protesters," Daphne suggested.

CLEAN ENERGY

FOSSIL FUELS POLLUTE

EMPLOYEES ONLY

FACT FILE

Some power plants use renewable energy. Hydroelectric plants use flowing water to make electricity. Solar plants take energy from the sun to make electricity. Wind farms turn wind energy into electricity. But even these plants can harm the environment.

"Could you tell us more about what you're protesting?" Velma asked.

"The burning of fossil fuels for energy pollutes the Earth," said a protester.

"Some local animals are becoming mutated from all the pollution," said another. "In fact, I just saw a mutated crocodile last week. The crocs are seeking revenge on the power plant."

"Is that true?" Velma asked a security guard. "Are mutant animals causing damage to the power plant?"

"I'm not allowed to comment," mumbled the security guard.

"We saw a mutated crocodile last night too," Daphne said. "Right after the power went out."

Scooby pointed to something moving in the bushes.

"I think we're about to get another look at that creepy croc!" shouted Shaggy.

"Like wow!" cried Shaggy. "I hope that crocodile isn't as hungry as I am!"

"It's leaving behind a trail of slime," noticed Velma.

"Follow that slime, gang!" Fred shouted. "We've got a mystery to solve!"

"The trail leads to the mayor's house," Daphne said. "Do you think he has something to do with this?"

"There's only one way to find out," Fred said. He knocked on the door.

"I was hoping he wouldn't say that," Shaggy moaned.

"Ronster!" Scooby shouted, pointing to the window.

"What's all the commotion about?" asked the mayor.

"Like, whew," said Shaggy. "We thought you were that gruesome gator."

"Actually, Mr. Mayor, we'd like to speak with you about what's happening at the power plant," said Velma.

"Come on, kids. We can talk in my study," said the mayor.

"Some really spooky stuff is going down at that power plant," said Shaggy. "We've been so busy investigating that we missed our snack break."

"There's no time for snacks," Fred said. "Mayor, the protesters said the plant is polluting local wildlife. Mutated crocodiles have been spotted all over town. And it seems as though they are damaging the plant."

"Perhaps our city should use renewable energy sources, Mayor," said Daphne. "They're safer and cause less pollution."

GROWL

"My family uses the sun to power our house," added Velma.

"Like, how can a sunburn power your house?" asked Shaggy.

"It's called solar power. Light from the sun can be used to make electricity," Velma explained. "Inside most solar panels are silicon crystals. When sunlight enters the panel, it knocks electrons from the silicon's atoms. The flow of these electrons creates electricity."

"Shaggy, is that your stomach growling?" asked Daphne.

"No—it's that re-volting crocodile!" shouted Shaggy.

"Re-rolting!" Scooby cried.

Daphne backed into a bookshelf. "Hey! These books are moving!"

"That's not a bookshelf," said Fred. "It's a door!"

"And it leads into a secret room," Velma said.

"The croc escaped out the window! Good riddance, reptile!" Shaggy yelled.

"This hatch leads to an underground tunnel," Fred said.

"Mayor, do you know anything about this?" Velma asked.

"I had no idea a tunnel existed under my house," the mayor insisted.

"A likely story," Shaggy muttered. "Well, we better run along."

"Not so fast," Daphne said. "Let's follow that tunnel and see where it leads."

"I already know where it leads," Shaggy said. **"To trouble."**

"Or to our next clue," Fred said. "We'll take it from here, Mayor."

"Uh oh," Shaggy said. "My flashlight's batteries, like, totally stopped working. Guess we better go home."

Scooby sniffed a pile of potatoes. "Rotatoes!" he said.

"Scooby-Doo found more potatoes," Daphne said. "How strange."

"And look at this, gang," Fred said. "I wonder what it is?"

"It's a homemade battery," explained Velma. "I made one in science class just last week."

"Potato power?" asked Shaggy. "How does that work?"

"First you push a zinc nail and a copper nail into the potato," Velma said. "The nails are electrodes. Electricity enters one electrode and leaves through the other."

"The potato acts like a conductor," Daphne said. "Electrons from the zinc's atoms flow through the potato to the copper's atoms."

"This electron transfer makes an electrical current," added Fred.

"That's groovy, but I'd rather make the potato into a French fry," Shaggy said.

"Re roo," Scooby agreed.

FACT FILE

Water is also a conductor, but the more pure the water is, the less it conducts. Fruits and vegetables work as conductors because the fluids inside of them create a circuit.

"Look!" Shaggy said. "Here's where the tunnel ends."

"Time to see where this circuit takes us," Fred said.

"Oh brother," Velma said.

"It leads to the power plant!" Fred said.

"Isn't this where that mutant croc came from?" Shaggy asked.

"Shaggy's right," Daphne said. "Something about this crocodile isn't adding up."

"I say we come back tonight," Velma suggested. "And we'll bring the mayor with us."

"Let's devise a trap," said Fred. "We'll use our brain power to solve this mystery."

That evening the mayor joined the gang back at the power plant.

"This is no time for a snack, Shaggy," Velma said.

"Scoob and I are using the delicious smell of fries to lure that far-out reptile," Shaggy said. "It seems to like potatoes, so it should love these French fries."

"Let's set up the trap," Fred said. "As soon as the crocodile crawls through the hatch, we'll lower the cage using this electric motor."

"You, like, made a motor?" Shaggy asked.

"We sure did," said Daphne. "It was easy. We looped insulated wire into a coil. Then we connected it to a large battery."

"When I hold this magnet above the coiled wire, it will spin," said Fred. "Remember that an electrical current creates a magnetic field. My magnet interacts with the magnetic field from the coiled wire to make it spin."

"For the sake of the town, I sure hope your idea works," said the mayor.

EMPLOYEES ONLY

"It's that cold-blooded beast!" shouted Shaggy.

"Now, gang!" Fred said, lifting the magnet over the wire.

"Now it's time to see who's beneath all those scales," said Velma.

Scooby removed the monster's mask.

"It's the security guard from the power plant!" Daphne said.

"Dale?" asked the mayor.

"Do you two, like, know each other?" asked Shaggy.

"This is Dale, my son," said the mayor. "What are you doing in that silly costume?"

"I've been sneaking information about the power plant to the news media," said Dale. "My friends and I wore the suits to scare everyone in town. This power plant causes pollution. We want to shut it down."

"Breaking the law isn't the right way to go about it," said the mayor.

"So, like, what was up with all those potatoes?" Shaggy said.

"Let me guess," Fred said. "Dale used them to make a battery. That's what powered his suit's glowing eyes."

"And I would've gotten away with it if it hadn't been for you meddling kids!" Dale said.

"Now that we've pulled the plug on this mystery, how about we go for burgers and fries? asked Daphne.

"You've, like, totally sparked my appetite!" Shaggy said.

"Rum!" agreed Scooby.

THE END

GLOSSARY

atom (AT-uhm)—the smallest particle of an element

conductor (kuhn-DUHK-tuhr)—material through which electric charges move easily; most conductors are metals

electricity (i-lek-TRIS-i-tee)—a natural force that can be used to make light and heat or to make machines work

electrode (eh-LEK-troad)—one of the two points through which electricity flows into and out of a battery

electron (i-LEK-tron)—a tiny particle in an atom that travels around the nucleus

fossil fuels (FAH-suhl FYOOLZ)—natural fuels formed from the remains of plants and animals; coal, oil, and natural gas are fossil fuels

generator (JEN-uh-ray-tur)—a machine that produces electricity by turning a magnet inside a coil of wire

insulator (IN-suh-late-ur)—material that keeps electricity inside wires or paths

magnetic field (mag-NET-ik FEELD)—the area around a magnet that has the power to attract magnetic metals

neutron (NOO-trahn)—particle in the nucleus of an atom that has no electric charge

nucleus (NOO-klee-uhss)—the center of an atom; a nucleus is made up of neutrons and protons

pollution (puh-LOO-shuhn)—harmful materials that damage the air, water, and soil

proton (PRO-tahn)—positively charged particle in the nucleus of an atom

solar power (SOH-lur POU-ur)—energy from the sun that can be used for heating and electricity

SCIENCE AND ENGINEERING PRACTICES

1. Asking questions (for science) and defining problems (for engineering)

2. Developing and using models

3. Planning and carrying out investigations

4. Analyzing and interpreting data

5. Using mathematics and computational thinking

6. Constructing explanations (for science) and designing solutions (for engineering)

7. Engaging in argument from evidence

8. Obtaining, evaluating, and communicating information

Next Generation Science Standards

READ MORE

Graham, Ian. *From Falling Water to Electric Car: An Energy Journey through the World of Electricity.* Energy Journeys. Chicago: Capstone Heinemann Library, 2015.

Hayes, Amy. *Freaky Stories about Electricity.* Freaky True Science. New York: Gareth Stevens Publishing, 2017.

Roland, James. *How Circuits Work.* Connect with Electricity. Minneapolis: Lerner Publications, 2017.

INTERNET SITES

FactHound offers a safe, fun way to find Internet sites related to this book. All of the sites on FactHound have been researched by our staff.

Here's all you do:

Visit *www.facthound.com*

Type in this code: 9781515736981

Check out projects, games and lots more at
www.capstonekids.com

INDEX

Thanks to our adviser for his expertise, research, and advice:
Paul Ohmann, PhD, Associate Professor of Physics
University of St. Thomas, St. Paul, Minnesota

Published in 2017 by Capstone Press, A Capstone Imprint
1710 Roe Crest Drive, North Mankato, Minnesota 56003
www.mycapstone.com

Library of Congress Cataloging-in-Publication Data
is available on the library of congress website.
ISBN: 978-1-5157-3698-1 (library hardcover)
978-1-5157-3702-5 (paperback)
978-1-5157-3714-8 (eBook PDF)
Summary: Jinkies! What happened to that crocodile? Scooby-Doo and the gang are
on a mission to find out what created the creepy crocodile ... and what the local power plant
might have to do with it. Join their investigation using the science of electricity to find the
shocking truth behind the mutant crocodile!

Editorial Credits
Editor: Kristen Mohn
Designer: Ashlee Suker
Creative Director: Nathan Gassman
Production Specialist: Laura Manthe
The illustrations in this book were created digitally.

Printed and bound in the USA.
010051S17

OTHER TITLES IN THIS SET: